LUXEMBOURG

21 THINGS TO DO IN 7 DAYS

1. Explore the historic Old Town of Luxembourg City

Nestled within the heart of Luxembourg, the historic Old Town of Luxembourg City is a captivating journey through centuries of rich history and culture. This UNESCO World Heritage Site is a testament to the city's resilience and charm.

Accessing the Old Town is seamless, with multiple entry points from various parts of the city. If arriving by train or bus, the central station provides easy access, and the Old Town is also reachable by car. Once there, visitors are welcomed by narrow cobblestone streets, medieval architecture, and an atmosphere that transports them to a bygone era.

Entrance to the Old Town is free, allowing for a budget-friendly exploration of its many wonders. Wander through the Place Guillaume II, the main square, where you'll find the Grand Ducal Palace. While entrance to the palace itself may require a ticket, the square is a hub of activity and a perfect starting point for your journey.

As you meander through the Old Town's labyrinthine streets, you'll encounter landmarks such as the Notre-Dame Cathedral and the Bock Casemates. The cathedral is a masterpiece of Gothic architecture, while the Bock Casemates offer a glimpse into the city's military history with an intricate network of underground tunnels.

Immerse yourself in the local culture by exploring Place d'Armes, a vibrant square surrounded by cafes and shops. Don't miss the opportunity to savor Luxembourgish cuisine at one of the many restaurants lining the streets.

The time required to explore the Old Town depends on your pace and the depth of exploration. A leisurely day can suffice, allowing you to absorb the ambiance, visit key landmarks, and indulge in local delights. To enhance your experience, consider guided tours that provide insights into the history and stories behind the Old Town's enchanting façades.

In essence, the historic Old Town of Luxembourg City offers a captivating journey through time, blending architectural marvels with the warmth of local hospitality.

2. Visit the Grand Ducal Palace

Nestled in the heart of Luxembourg City, the Grand Ducal Palace stands as a symbol of the country's rich history and serves as the official residence of the Grand Duke of Luxembourg. A visit to this architectural gem provides a unique opportunity to witness the grandeur of Luxembourg's monarchy and its cultural significance.

Access to the Grand Ducal Palace is convenient, situated in the heart of the Old Town. Whether you're arriving by foot, public transport, or car, the central location ensures easy accessibility. The palace is often part of guided walking tours that explore the historical treasures of Luxembourg City.

While exploring the exterior of the Grand Ducal Palace is a delightful experience on its own, entry to the interior may require a ticket. The ticket prices can vary, and visitors are advised to check the official website or local tourism offices for the latest information. Some tours offer combined tickets that include access to multiple attractions, providing excellent value for those eager to explore further.

Inside the palace, marvel at the opulent state rooms adorned with magnificent tapestries, ornate furniture, and historical artifacts. Knowledgeable guides or audio tours often accompany visitors, offering insights into the palace's history and the role it plays in Luxembourg's constitutional monarchy.

A visit to the Grand Ducal Palace typically takes around one to two hours, allowing ample time to appreciate the intricate details of the architecture and absorb the regal atmosphere. Photography is often allowed in designated areas, so be sure to capture the grandeur of this iconic landmark.

To make the most of your visit, consider timing your exploration with the changing of the guard ceremony, a ceremonial display that adds a touch of pageantry to the overall experience. The Grand Ducal Palace, with its blend of history and grandeur, stands as a must-see destination for those seeking a glimpse into Luxembourg's royal legacy.

3. Wander through the Bock Casemates, an underground fortress

Embark on a fascinating journey through time as you explore the Bock Casemates, an underground fortress that weaves through the history of Luxembourg. Nestled in the heart of Luxembourg City, this intricate network of tunnels and chambers has played a pivotal role in the country's defense for centuries.

Accessible by foot, the Bock Casemates are conveniently located in the historic Old Town of Luxembourg City. Visitors can easily reach the site through a leisurely stroll or as part of guided walking tours that uncover the city's rich cultural heritage.

To delve into the depths of this subterranean marvel, a ticket is required. Prices may vary, so it's advisable to check the official website or inquire at local tourism offices for the latest information. Some tour packages offer combined tickets for multiple attractions, providing an excellent opportunity to explore various historical sites.

As you descend into the Bock Casemates, be prepared to be transported back in time. The labyrinthine tunnels and chambers served as a military stronghold and shelter during times of conflict. The immersive experience is enhanced by informative guides or audio tours that recount the fascinating stories of the fortress and its strategic significance.

Allow at least one to two hours for your exploration, giving you ample time to navigate the extensive underground passages and absorb the historical narratives. The temperature inside the casemates remains relatively constant, so dress comfortably for your subterranean adventure.

Marvel at the architecture and engineering ingenuity that went into creating this underground fortress, with its defense mechanisms and strategic positioning. Photography is generally permitted, allowing you to capture the unique atmosphere and historical details that define the Bock Casemates.

For an added touch of authenticity, consider visiting during special events or guided night tours, which provide a different perspective on this remarkable historical site. The Bock Casemates stand as a testament to Luxembourg's resilience and are a must-visit destination for history enthusiasts and curious travelers alike.

4. Enjoy the views from the Corniche, a picturesque promenade

Discover the breathtaking beauty of Luxembourg by strolling along the Corniche, a picturesque promenade that offers panoramic views of the Alzette River and the enchanting Lower Town. This iconic spot is renowned for its scenic charm and provides an excellent vantage point to appreciate the city's stunning landscapes.

The Corniche is easily accessible, situated atop the city's historic fortifications. You can reach this elevated promenade by walking from the Old Town or taking scenic routes that wind through the charming streets of Luxembourg City. No tickets are required to enjoy the views from the Corniche, making it a delightful and budget-friendly experience for all.

As you amble along the promenade, take in the postcard-perfect scenes of the Alzette River winding through the valley below. The panoramic vistas include charming bridges, historic buildings, and the verdant landscapes that define Luxembourg's captivating allure.

Whether you choose to explore the Corniche during the day or as the sun begins to set, the experience is equally enchanting. Allow yourself at least an hour to leisurely stroll along the promenade, capturing the beauty of the surroundings and pausing to appreciate the scenic overlooks.

While there are no specific activities or attractions along the Corniche, the real charm lies in the serene ambiance and the opportunity to unwind amidst nature's beauty. Photographers will find ample inspiration, and couples seeking a romantic setting will be captivated by the romantic atmosphere.

Consider packing a picnic or stopping by one of the nearby cafes to savor a moment of relaxation with a backdrop of Luxembourg's captivating vistas. The Corniche is an ideal spot for introspection, leisurely walks, or simply enjoying the company of friends and family in a tranquil setting.
Whether you're a solo traveler seeking solitude or part of a group looking for a serene escape, the Corniche promises an unforgettable experience, leaving you with cherished memories of Luxembourg's natural splendor.

5. Discover the Notre-Dame Cathedral

Embark on a cultural journey in Luxembourg by visiting the Notre-Dame Cathedral, a magnificent architectural gem that stands as a symbol of the city's rich history and religious heritage.

Situated in the heart of Luxembourg City, the Notre-Dame Cathedral is easily accessible from various points in the city center. Whether you prefer a leisurely stroll through the charming streets or a convenient public transport option, reaching this iconic landmark is a seamless experience.

Entry to the Notre-Dame Cathedral is free, allowing visitors to explore its awe-inspiring interiors without the need for tickets. As you step inside, marvel at the grandeur of Gothic architecture, intricate stained glass windows, and the serene atmosphere that envelopes this sacred space. Take your time to wander through the nave, admire the impressive organ, and reflect in the tranquility of the cathedral. Guided tours are available for those seeking a deeper understanding of the historical and religious significance of the Notre-Dame Cathedral.

The suggested duration for a visit to the cathedral is approximately one hour. This allows ample time to appreciate the architectural details, soak in the spiritual ambiance, and perhaps attend a religious service if timing aligns with the schedule.

If you're an art enthusiast, don't miss the opportunity to view the various sculptures and artworks housed within the cathedral. Each piece contributes to the overall cultural and artistic richness of this sacred space.

Before or after your visit, take a moment to explore the surrounding area. Luxembourg's Old Town is known for its charming cafes, boutique shops, and historical landmarks, creating a delightful ambiance for leisurely walks and exploration.

Whether you're a history buff, architecture enthusiast, or someone seeking a peaceful escape, the Notre-Dame Cathedral offers a profound and enriching experience. Immerse yourself in the cultural tapestry of Luxembourg as you explore this iconic religious monument.

6. Stroll around Place d'Armes for cafes and shops

Embark on a leisurely adventure in Luxembourg City by strolling around Place d'Armes, a charming square nestled in the heart of the Old Town. Easily reachable from various points in the city center, this lively square serves as a hub for both locals and visitors seeking a delightful blend of cafes, shops, and vibrant ambiance.

Place d'Armes is conveniently located, making it accessible by foot or public transport. Whether you're exploring the winding streets of the Old Town or arriving from other parts of the city, you'll find the square to be a central meeting point.

The best part? There's no need for tickets to enter Place d'Armes. This public square welcomes everyone with open arms, inviting you to experience the lively atmosphere and immerse yourself in the local culture.

Upon arriving, let your senses guide you as you explore the array of cafes lining the square. Choose a quaint outdoor terrace to savor a cup of freshly brewed coffee or indulge in a delectable pastry. The cafes offer the perfect vantage point for people-watching and soaking in the relaxed Luxembourgish lifestyle.

As you meander through Place d'Armes, take the opportunity to browse the boutique shops that adorn the square. From charming bookstores to chic boutiques, you'll discover a variety of unique finds, making it an ideal spot for souvenir shopping or simply enjoying the local retail scene.

The suggested duration for a leisurely stroll around Place d'Armes is flexible, allowing you to set your own pace. Whether you're looking for a quick visit or planning to spend a lazy afternoon, the square caters to diverse preferences.

Immerse yourself in the vibrant energy of Place d'Armes, where the fusion of historic charm and contemporary allure creates a truly enchanting experience. Whether you're sipping coffee, exploring shops, or simply enjoying the ambiance, this iconic square promises a memorable and delightful sojourn in Luxembourg City.

7. Explore the Mudam (Musée d'Art Moderne Grand-Duc Jean)

Embark on a captivating artistic journey at the Mudam (Musée d'Art Moderne Grand-Duc Jean), Luxembourg's premier contemporary art museum. Situated in the Kirchberg district, the Mudam is easily accessible from the city center, offering a unique blend of modern architecture and cutting-edge art.

To reach Mudam, you can opt for a scenic walk from the Old Town, take public transportation, or utilize other convenient modes of travel. The museum's striking design, envisioned by architect I. M. Pei, makes it a landmark in itself.

Upon arrival, purchase tickets to enter the museum. The entrance fee is a reasonable investment in experiencing a diverse range of contemporary artworks from both established and emerging artists. Check the museum's official website for updated ticket prices and any special exhibitions that might enhance your visit.

Inside Mudam, immerse yourself in the world of contemporary art across various mediums. Explore thought-provoking installations, avant-garde sculptures, and boundary-pushing paintings. The museum's collection is dynamic, featuring works that challenge traditional perspectives and evoke meaningful dialogues.

Take your time to wander through the different exhibition spaces, each curated to provide a unique encounter with the artistic expressions of our time. Whether you're an art enthusiast or a casual visitor, Mudam offers engaging experiences for all.

The suggested duration for exploring Mudam is flexible, ranging from a couple of hours to a half-day, depending on your level of interest and engagement with the exhibits. Take breaks at the museum's cafe, which often features panoramic views of the surrounding Kirchberg area. Before your visit, check the Mudam website for any temporary exhibitions, guided tours, or special events that might align with your interests. Whether you're delving into the world of contemporary art for the first time or expanding your artistic horizons, Mudam promises an enriching and visually stimulating experience in the heart of Luxembourg.

8. Visit the National Museum of History and Art

Embark on a captivating journey through Luxembourg's rich history at the National Museum of History and Art, located in the heart of the capital city. The museum, often referred to as MNHA, offers a comprehensive exploration of Luxembourg's cultural heritage, spanning from prehistoric times to the contemporary era.

The National Museum of History and Art is conveniently situated near the Fish Market Square, making it easily accessible on foot from the city center. Alternatively, you can utilize public transportation, such as buses, to reach this cultural gem.

Upon arrival, purchase tickets to gain access to the museum's diverse exhibits. The entrance fee is reasonable and provides visitors with an in-depth look at Luxembourg's historical evolution. Check the official website for the most up-to-date ticket prices and any temporary exhibitions that may enhance your visit.

Inside MNHA, discover a wealth of artifacts, artworks, and archaeological findings. The museum's collections are thoughtfully curated to present Luxembourg's history in a chronological and thematic manner. Explore galleries dedicated to archaeology, fine arts, and decorative arts, among others.

Take your time to absorb the fascinating details within each exhibition. Engage with artifacts ranging from ancient tools to medieval manuscripts, and marvel at the artistic achievements that reflect Luxembourg's cultural identity.

The suggested duration for a visit to MNHA can vary, but plan for at least a couple of hours to fully appreciate the exhibits. Take advantage of the museum's educational programs, guided tours, or audio guides to enhance your understanding of the displays.

Before your visit, check the museum's schedule for any special events, lectures, or temporary exhibitions that align with your interests. MNHA stands as a testament to Luxembourg's rich cultural tapestry, offering a captivating and educational experience for visitors eager to delve into the nation's storied past.

9. Walk through the Grund district along the Alzette River

Embark on a picturesque stroll through Luxembourg's enchanting Grund district, nestled along the serene Alzette River. This historic neighborhood, with its cobblestone streets and charming architecture, provides a delightful escape into the heart of Luxembourg City.

The Grund district is conveniently located near the city center, making it easily accessible on foot. Simply follow the signs from the Place Guillaume II or the Palais Grand-Ducal, and you'll soon find yourself immersed in the inviting ambiance of the Grund.

There is no admission fee to explore the Grund district, making it an accessible and budget-friendly activity for tourists. This allows you to wander freely through the narrow lanes and absorb the unique atmosphere without any financial constraints.

As you traverse the Grund, take in the scenic views of the Alzette River, which meanders through the district, adding to its charm. Capture the postcard-perfect scenes of colorful houses, quaint bridges, and the gentle flow of the river. The area is particularly enchanting during the warmer months when outdoor cafés along the riverbanks invite you to pause and savor the moment.

The recommended duration for a leisurely walk through the Grund district is approximately 1 to 2 hours, allowing ample time for exploration, photography, and perhaps a stop at a local café. However, feel free to adjust your pace based on your preferences and interests.

Immerse yourself in the district's history by visiting notable landmarks like the Neumünster Abbey, a cultural and meeting center with a rich heritage. Explore the small squares and alleys that reveal hidden gems, such as art galleries, boutique shops, and cozy eateries.

Before your visit, check for any local events or festivals taking place in the Grund, as these can add an extra layer of excitement to your experience. Whether you're a history enthusiast, an architecture admirer, or simply seeking a peaceful riverside escape, a walk through the Grund district promises a delightful and enriching adventure in Luxembourg City.

10. Admire the modern architecture of the European Court of Justice

Embark on a captivating journey through Luxembourg City to admire the modern architecture of the European Court of Justice, a prominent institution in the heart of the European Union. The European Court of Justice is located in the Kirchberg district, a short distance from the city center.

To reach this architectural marvel, you can easily take a taxi, use public transportation, or enjoy a scenic walk from the city center. The Kirchberg area is well-connected, and signs will guide you to the European Court of Justice, an iconic symbol of the EU's judicial authority.

One of the noteworthy aspects of this attraction is that admission is typically free. Visitors are welcome to explore the exterior of the building, marvel at its striking design, and appreciate its significance on the European stage. The modern and innovative architecture of the European Court of Justice reflects the values and ideals of the European Union.

Upon arrival, take your time to walk around the exterior of the building, capturing the impressive angles and contemporary aesthetic. The vast esplanade in front of the Court provides an ideal vantage point for admiring the structure and taking photographs. The building's sleek lines and glass façade create a visually stunning and symbolic representation of transparency and openness.

While you cannot enter the courtrooms without prior arrangement, the exterior alone offers a compelling experience for architecture enthusiasts and those interested in the European Union's institutions. Consider visiting during the day to fully appreciate the play of natural light on the building's surfaces.

The recommended duration for this visit is approximately 1 to 1.5 hours, allowing you ample time to explore the surroundings, absorb the architectural details, and perhaps enjoy a leisurely stroll in the nearby Parc Central.

Before your visit, check for any special events or guided tours that may enhance your understanding of the European Court of Justice and its role in the EU. This excursion promises not only a visual feast for architecture lovers but also a meaningful encounter with the EU's legal foundation in Luxembourg City.

11. Discover the Philharmonie Luxembourg for concerts and events

Embark on a harmonious journey at the Philharmonie Luxembourg, a cultural gem where music aficionados and enthusiasts converge for exquisite concerts and events. Nestled in the Kirchberg district of Luxembourg City, this iconic venue is easily accessible, offering a memorable experience for visitors.

Getting to the Philharmonie Luxembourg is convenient, with various transportation options available. Whether you prefer a taxi, public transport, or a leisurely walk, signs will guide you to this architectural masterpiece. The Philharmonie is situated in close proximity to the European institutions, adding to the allure of the Kirchberg area.

Ticket prices for concerts and events at the Philharmonie Luxembourg vary depending on the performance, seating arrangement, and artist. It's advisable to check the official website or visit the box office for detailed information on upcoming events, schedules, and ticket prices. Booking tickets in advance is recommended, especially for popular performances.

Upon entering the Philharmonie, you'll be immersed in a world of artistic excellence and acoustic brilliance. The state-of-the-art concert hall is renowned for its exceptional acoustics, creating an intimate and captivating atmosphere for every performance. Take time to explore the interior architecture, designed to complement the auditory experience.

The duration of your visit will depend on the event you attend. Concerts and performances typically last between 1.5 to 2 hours, providing an enchanting evening filled with musical delights. Before your visit, consider researching the program to familiarize yourself with the repertoire and artists.

Enhance your experience by arriving early to savor the ambiance of the Philharmonie and perhaps enjoy a pre-concert drink in the foyer. Some events may offer post-concert talks or meet-the-artist sessions, providing additional insights into the world of classical and contemporary music.

The Philharmonie Luxembourg stands as a testament to Luxembourg's commitment to cultural enrichment. Whether you are a seasoned classical music enthusiast or a newcomer to the symphonic world, a visit to the Philharmonie promises an unforgettable encounter with the power and beauty of live music in the heart of Luxembourg City.

12. Experience the Luxembourg American Cemetery and Memorial

Embark on a poignant journey to the Luxembourg American Cemetery and Memorial, a solemn tribute to the sacrifices made during World War II. Situated in Hamm, a suburb of Luxembourg City, this hallowed ground provides a serene and reflective atmosphere.

Accessing the Luxembourg American Cemetery is straightforward, with multiple transportation options available. Whether by car, public transport, or organized tours, visitors can easily reach the site. Ample parking is available for those opting to drive, and well-marked paths guide pedestrians to the entrance.

Entrance to the cemetery is free, reflecting the site's role as a memorial and a symbol of gratitude. It is recommended to check the official website or visitor center for any guided tours or events that may enhance your understanding of the history and significance of the memorial.

Upon arrival, you'll be greeted by the breathtaking sight of row upon row of white crosses and Stars of David, honoring the 5,076 American service members laid to rest here. Take a moment to appreciate the meticulously maintained grounds and the solemnity that pervades the area.

While strolling through the cemetery, consider visiting the memorial chapel. The chapel features a beautiful mosaic map depicting military operations during the Battle of the Bulge, offering historical context to the site. Additionally, the Walls of the Missing bear the names of 371 soldiers whose remains were never recovered.

Exploring the Luxembourg American Cemetery is a contemplative experience that may take approximately 1 to 2 hours. Take your time to pay respects, read the inscriptions on the markers, and absorb the historical significance of this sacred place.

Before leaving, pause at the visitor center, which provides additional information, exhibits, and a chance to reflect on the profound impact of war. The Luxembourg American Cemetery and Memorial stands as a testament to the enduring bond between Luxembourg and the United States, commemorating the bravery and sacrifice of those who fought for freedom.

13. Hike or bike in Mullerthal, the "Little Switzerland" of Luxembourg

Embark on an exhilarating adventure in Mullerthal, fondly known as the "Little Switzerland" of Luxembourg, where picturesque landscapes and winding trails await outdoor enthusiasts. This natural gem is renowned for its stunning rock formations, dense forests, and meandering streams, offering a perfect escape into Luxembourg's scenic beauty.

Getting to Mullerthal is accessible by car, and there are also public transportation options available. Once there, no entrance fees are required to explore the natural wonders of Mullerthal, making it an ideal destination for budget-conscious travelers.

Begin your journey at the Mullerthal Trail, a well-marked network of hiking and biking paths that lead you through the heart of this enchanting region. The trails vary in difficulty, catering to both novice and experienced hikers or bikers. Whether you choose the challenging routes that lead to panoramic viewpoints or opt for more leisurely paths, the trails offer an immersive experience into Luxembourg's diverse terrain.

The Mullerthal Trail is divided into several loops, allowing you to customize your adventure based on your preferences and time constraints. A suggested trail, such as the Mullerthal Trail Extra Tour 2, takes you through iconic rock formations like the "Schiessentümpel" waterfall and the unique rock labyrinth known as the "Heringer Millen."

The duration of your exploration in Mullerthal can vary based on the chosen trail and your pace. A half-day to a full day is recommended to fully appreciate the natural beauty and tranquility of the area.

As you traverse the trails, immerse yourself in the lush greenery, discover hidden caves and cliffs, and relish the serenity of the bubbling streams. Don't forget to bring comfortable footwear, a camera to capture the breathtaking scenery, and snacks to enjoy a picnic amid nature's embrace.

Before embarking on your Mullerthal adventure, check the weather conditions and trail statuses for a safe and enjoyable experience in this captivating corner of Luxembourg.

14. Visit Vianden Castle in the Ardennes

Uncover the rich history and architectural splendor of Vianden Castle, an iconic fortress nestled in the heart of the Ardennes region in Luxembourg. Vianden Castle, perched atop a hill overlooking the charming town of Vianden, is a testament to medieval grandeur and offers visitors a journey back in time.

To reach Vianden Castle, you can take a scenic drive through the Ardennes or opt for public transportation, including buses or guided tours. The castle is open to the public, and tickets can be purchased on-site or online. Prices may vary based on age and whether you choose to explore the castle and its exhibits independently or with a guided tour.

Upon arrival, marvel at the castle's imposing towers and well-preserved fortifications. The interior of Vianden Castle is a treasure trove of medieval artifacts, period furniture, and exhibits that provide insight into the castle's storied past. Explore the various rooms, including the chapel, dining hall, and knight's chamber, each showcasing a different facet of medieval life.

For an enriching experience, consider joining a guided tour led by knowledgeable staff who share captivating stories about the castle's history and its former inhabitants. Learn about the Counts of Vianden and the role the castle played in the region's defense and cultural development.

The duration of your visit to Vianden Castle can vary based on your level of interest and whether you choose to explore the castle grounds and surrounding areas. Plan for a half-day to a full day to fully appreciate the historical significance and architectural beauty of this medieval gem.

As you wander through the castle's courtyards and ramparts, savor panoramic views of the Ardennes and the picturesque town below. Capture the breathtaking scenery, and don't forget to visit the castle's gift shop, where you can find souvenirs to commemorate your visit.

Before heading to Vianden Castle, check the castle's official website for the latest information on opening hours, special events, and guidelines to ensure a seamless and enjoyable visit.

15. Explore the Luxembourg City History Museum

Embark on a captivating journey through time by exploring the Luxembourg City History Museum, a cultural gem that unravels the rich tapestry of Luxembourg's past. Located in the heart of Luxembourg City, this museum provides a comprehensive overview of the country's history, from its medieval origins to the present day.

Getting to the Luxembourg City History Museum is convenient, as it is situated in the city center. Visitors can easily reach it by public transportation, such as buses or taxis. The museum is generally open to the public, and tickets can be purchased on-site or through their official website. Admission prices may vary based on factors such as age, student status, and whether you prefer a guided tour.

Upon entering the museum, immerse yourself in the engaging exhibits that showcase Luxembourg's evolution over the centuries. Explore artifacts, documents, and multimedia displays that depict key historical events, cultural milestones, and the diverse heritage of the Luxembourgish people.

To enhance your visit, consider participating in a guided tour offered by the museum. Knowledgeable guides provide valuable insights, anecdotes, and context, making the historical narrative come to life. The museum's thematic sections cover topics ranging from medieval times and the impact of wars to the development of Luxembourg as a modern European city.

Plan for a leisurely visit, as the Luxembourg City History Museum offers a wealth of information to absorb. Depending on your level of interest, a visit may take a few hours. Take your time to explore each section thoroughly, gaining a deeper understanding of Luxembourg's unique identity.

Before your visit, check the museum's official website for the latest information on opening hours, any special exhibitions, and guidelines. Don't miss the opportunity to delve into Luxembourg's fascinating history and heritage at this esteemed cultural institution.

16. Take a scenic drive through the Luxembourgish countryside

Embark on an enchanting journey through the picturesque Luxembourgish countryside with a scenic drive that promises breathtaking landscapes and charming villages. This self-guided adventure offers a refreshing escape into the heart of nature, allowing you to immerse yourself in the beauty that Luxembourg's rural areas have to offer.

Getting to the starting point of your scenic drive is easy, as Luxembourg boasts a well-connected road network. Whether you're renting a car or using your own, plan your route to include the quaint villages and rolling hills that characterize the Luxembourgish countryside.

No tickets are required for this scenic drive, making it an affordable and flexible option for travelers. Begin your journey at your preferred time, and take advantage of the freedom to stop and explore whenever a captivating scene captures your attention.

As you traverse the winding roads, witness the changing landscapes that range from lush green meadows to dense forests and meandering rivers. Pass through charming villages adorned with traditional houses and discover hidden gems along the way.

Take the opportunity to visit local cafes or roadside stalls to savor Luxembourgish treats and delicacies. Enjoy a leisurely pace, allowing the beauty of the countryside to unfold at every turn. Consider including iconic landmarks like Vianden Castle or the Mullerthal region in your route for added cultural and natural highlights.

The duration of the scenic drive depends on your chosen route and how much time you dedicate to exploring each stop. Plan for a full day to truly appreciate the tranquility and serenity of the Luxembourgish countryside.

Before embarking on your journey, ensure your vehicle is in good condition, and have a map or navigation system on hand. Check the weather forecast for optimal driving conditions, and don't forget your camera to capture the breathtaking vistas along the way. Experience the idyllic charm of Luxembourg's countryside on this memorable scenic drive.

17. Wander through the Kirchberg district for modern architecture

Embark on a captivating exploration of Luxembourg's modern architecture by wandering through the dynamic Kirchberg district. Home to striking contemporary structures, this district is a testament to Luxembourg's commitment to innovation and design.

Getting to Kirchberg is convenient, thanks to Luxembourg City's efficient public transportation system. Bus services and trams connect the city center to Kirchberg, providing an easy and affordable means of travel. If you prefer walking, the district is accessible from the city center, offering a scenic journey.

No tickets are required to explore the Kirchberg district, making it an accessible and budget-friendly activity. As you stroll through the area, marvel at the impressive architectural marvels that define the skyline. Notable landmarks include the European Court of Justice, the European Investment Bank, and the Philharmonie Luxembourg.

Take the time to appreciate the unique designs and structures, capturing the essence of modern Luxembourgish architecture. Many buildings are set amidst beautifully landscaped areas, creating a harmonious blend of nature and urbanity.

Consider visiting the Philharmonie Luxembourg, a renowned concert hall known for its distinctive contemporary design. Check the schedule for performances or, if time allows, take a guided tour to gain insights into the architectural and cultural significance of this iconic venue.

The duration of your wander through the Kirchberg district depends on your pace and the sites you choose to explore. Plan for at least a half-day to thoroughly enjoy the architectural wonders and perhaps indulge in a leisurely meal at one of the district's stylish cafes or restaurants.

Before setting out, ensure you have comfortable walking shoes, a camera to capture the innovative designs, and a map or smartphone for navigation. Kirchberg invites you to immerse yourself in Luxembourg's modern aesthetic, providing a captivating juxtaposition to the city's historical charm.

18. Experience the Luxembourg City Film Festival

Immerse yourself in the world of cinema by experiencing the Luxembourg City Film Festival, a cultural celebration that brings together film enthusiasts from around the globe. Delve into the rich tapestry of cinematic artistry in the heart of Luxembourg City.

Getting to the Luxembourg City Film Festival is straightforward, as it typically takes place in various venues within the city center. Public transportation, including buses and trams, is readily available, ensuring easy access. Check the festival's official website or local event listings for venue details and specific film screenings.

Ticket prices for the Luxembourg City Film Festival vary depending on the type of screening and any associated events. Festival organizers often offer a range of ticket options, including single screening tickets and passes for multiple films. Purchase tickets in advance through the festival's official website or designated ticket outlets.

Upon arrival, immerse yourself in a diverse selection of films, including international features, documentaries, and shorts. The Luxembourg City Film Festival is known for its inclusive programming, showcasing a broad spectrum of genres and styles. Attendees have the opportunity to engage with filmmakers, actors, and fellow cinephiles during Q&A sessions and panel discussions.

The duration of your experience at the film festival depends on your schedule and the number of screenings you plan to attend. With numerous films on offer, consider dedicating a day or more to fully appreciate the cinematic offerings.

To make the most of your time, explore nearby cafes or restaurants for a quick bite between screenings. Luxembourg City's central location allows for easy exploration of the surrounding areas, providing additional opportunities for sightseeing and cultural immersion.

Before attending, check the festival's schedule, film lineup, and any special events or exhibitions. Bring comfortable clothing, as you may spend extended periods in screening rooms, and consider a small notebook or a smartphone for jotting down your thoughts and recommendations.

The Luxembourg City Film Festival promises an enriching cinematic journey, offering a unique blend of international and local perspectives within the vibrant cultural landscape of Luxembourg City.

19. Enjoy a boat tour on the Moselle River

Embark on a picturesque adventure by enjoying a boat tour on the Moselle River, a serene waterway that winds through the charming Luxembourgish countryside. This experience promises a tranquil escape, providing stunning views of vineyard-covered hills and historic villages along the riverbanks.

Getting to the starting point of the boat tour is convenient, with several launching locations along the Moselle River. Popular departure points include Remich and Grevenmacher, both easily accessible by car or public transportation. Check with local tour operators or the tourist information center for details on specific departure points and available tours.

Ticket prices for boat tours on the Moselle River vary depending on the tour duration and services offered. Tickets can often be purchased directly from the tour operator or through the tourist information center. Consider opting for guided tours that provide insights into the region's history, culture, and winemaking traditions.

Once on board, surrender to the tranquility of the Moselle River as you glide through the water. Most boat tours offer open-air seating, allowing you to fully immerse yourself in the natural beauty of the surroundings. Captivating landscapes, vineyards, and quaint villages will unfold before your eyes.

The duration of a typical boat tour on the Moselle River ranges from one to several hours. Choose a tour that aligns with your preferences, whether you're seeking a leisurely cruise or a more comprehensive exploration of the region. Some tours may include stops at local wineries, allowing you to sample Luxembourg's renowned wines.

To enhance your experience, pack essentials such as sunscreen, a hat, and comfortable clothing. Consider bringing a camera to capture the scenic beauty along the river. Many boat operators offer refreshments on board, but you may also want to bring water and snacks. Immerse yourself in the idyllic landscapes and cultural richness that the Moselle River offers. Whether you're a nature enthusiast, wine lover, or simply seeking relaxation, a boat tour on the Moselle River provides a delightful escape into Luxembourg's enchanting countryside.

20. Visit the Vianden Chairlift for panoramic views

Embark on an exhilarating journey to the Vianden Chairlift for breathtaking panoramic views of the enchanting Luxembourgish landscape. This iconic chairlift, situated in the picturesque town of Vianden, promises an unforgettable experience with its stunning vistas and convenient accessibility.

Getting to the Vianden Chairlift is a straightforward venture. Vianden is well-connected by road, and ample parking is available near the chairlift station. Additionally, public transportation options may be available, allowing you to seamlessly reach this scenic spot. Check with local transport authorities for the latest schedules and routes.

Upon arrival, purchase tickets for the chairlift, which typically offer a round-trip experience. Ticket prices vary, and discounts may be available for children or groups, so it's advisable to check with the ticket office for the latest information. The ticket purchase often includes the cost of the chairlift ride and access to the observation platform at the top.

Board the chairlift and ascend gracefully over the lush landscapes surrounding Vianden. The gentle ascent provides a unique perspective of the town, the meandering Our River, and the Luxembourg Ardennes. As you ascend, anticipate breathtaking views unfolding beneath you, creating a memorable and Instagram-worthy experience.

Upon reaching the summit, spend time at the observation platform absorbing the panoramic vistas. The expansive views of the Our Valley, Vianden Castle, and the surrounding verdant hills showcase the natural beauty that Luxembourg is renowned for. Capture the scenic beauty through photographs or simply relish the moment of tranquility.

The Vianden Chairlift experience can take approximately 20-30 minutes, allowing you to savor the landscapes at a leisurely pace. To enhance your visit, consider bringing a camera, comfortable walking shoes, and weather-appropriate clothing, especially if you plan to explore the area further.

Whether you're a nature enthusiast, a photography enthusiast, or simply seeking a serene escape, the Vianden Chairlift offers a remarkable experience. Revel in the beauty of Luxembourg's landscapes as you glide through the air, creating memories that will linger long after your visit.

21. Explore the charming village of Echternach

Embark on a delightful journey to the charming village of Echternach, nestled in the heart of Luxembourg. Renowned for its historical significance, natural beauty, and cultural richness, Echternach offers a captivating experience for travelers seeking a blend of heritage and tranquility.

Getting to Echternach is convenient, with various transportation options available. The village is accessible by car, and ample parking facilities are typically available. If you prefer public transportation, buses or other local services may connect you to Echternach from nearby towns. Check the latest schedules and routes for a seamless journey.

Echternach is renowned for its historical sites, including the stunning Echternach Abbey. Entrance fees may apply, and guided tours could enhance your understanding of the abbey's rich history and architectural significance. Check with the abbey's administration for the latest information on opening hours and ticket prices.

Wander through the enchanting streets of Echternach and explore its cozy cafes, boutique shops, and picturesque squares. The village exudes a timeless charm, with well-preserved medieval architecture and a welcoming atmosphere. Take your time to absorb the local ambiance and perhaps indulge in some authentic Luxembourgish cuisine at one of the local eateries.

Don't miss the opportunity to visit the beautiful Echternach Lake, a serene spot offering scenic views and a peaceful environment. Whether you prefer a leisurely stroll around the lake or a moment of relaxation by its shores, the lake provides a tranquil escape.

If you're visiting Echternach during the spring, consider timing your visit with the famous Echternach Dancing Procession, an UNESCO-listed event. This unique folkloric tradition attracts visitors from around the world and adds a cultural dimension to your experience. Check the event schedule and plan accordingly.

The duration of your visit to Echternach can vary based on your interests. Exploring the village and its key attractions, including the abbey and the lake, can be accomplished in a day. However, if you wish to delve deeper into the cultural and historical aspects, extending your stay may be worthwhile.

Remember to wear comfortable shoes for exploring the village's cobblestone streets and consider bringing a camera to capture the picturesque moments.

When visiting Luxembourg here are 7 valuable pieces of advice to keep in mind:

1. Cultural Etiquette: Respect local customs and traditions. Luxembourg has a rich cultural heritage, and politeness is highly valued. Greet locals with a friendly "Moien" (hello) and be mindful of social norms.

2. Multilingual Atmosphere: Luxembourg is a multilingual country with Luxembourgish, French, and German being widely spoken. English is also commonly understood. Familiarize yourself with basic phrases in these languages to enhance your communication.

3. Public Transportation: Public transportation is efficient and well-connected. Consider using buses and trains to explore the country comfortably. The Luxembourg Card provides unlimited access to public transport and free entry to many attractions.

4. Currency and Payments: Luxembourg uses the Euro (EUR). Credit cards are widely accepted, but it's advisable to have some cash on hand, especially in rural areas. ATMs are readily available in urban centers.

5. Weather Preparedness: Luxembourg experiences a temperate climate, so pack accordingly. Check the weather forecast before your trip and bring layers, as temperatures can vary. A waterproof jacket and comfortable walking shoes are advisable for exploring.

6. Safety Measures: Luxembourg is known for its safety, but it's wise to remain vigilant. Keep an eye on your belongings, especially in crowded tourist areas. The emergency number is 112 for police, fire, and medical assistance.

7. Explore Nature: Luxembourg boasts stunning natural landscapes. Take advantage of hiking and biking trails in places like Mullerthal ("Little Switzerland") and the Ardennes. Respect nature and follow designated paths to preserve the environment.

Remember to savor the local cuisine, which often combines French and German influences. Enjoy Luxembourg's diverse offerings, from its historic sites to its vibrant contemporary culture.

Here are 7 of the best services to consider using:

1. Vël'OK Bike Sharing: Explore Luxembourg City on two wheels with Vël'OK bike-sharing services. Conveniently located stations allow you to pick up and drop off bikes, providing a sustainable and enjoyable way to see the city.

2. Luxembourg Card for Tourists: The Luxembourg Card offers unlimited access to public transportation, including buses and trains, and provides free entry to numerous museums and attractions across the country. It's a cost-effective way to explore.

3. Nomad Space Co-Working: If you need a workspace while traveling, consider Nomad Space co-working facilities. These shared offices provide a professional environment with modern amenities for remote workers and digital nomads.

4. Webtaxi Luxembourg: For hassle-free transportation, Webtaxi Luxembourg offers reliable taxi services. Book a taxi online or through their app to conveniently navigate the city or travel to surrounding areas.

5. Docler Holding Fitness Centers: Stay active during your visit by using the fitness centers operated by Docler Holding. These facilities provide modern equipment and wellness services for both residents and visitors.

6. Satellite Navigation Apps: Utilize navigation apps like Google Maps or Waze to efficiently move around Luxembourg. These apps offer real-time traffic updates and directions, ensuring a smooth travel experience.

7. Luxembourg Airport Lounges: If you're flying into or out of Luxembourg, consider using airport lounges for a more comfortable and relaxing experience. Enjoy amenities like complimentary snacks, beverages, and Wi-Fi.

These services cater to various needs, from transportation and workspaces to fitness and navigation, enhancing your overall experience in Luxembourg.

Top 7 Must-Try Dining Spots in Luxembourg:

1. Mosconi: Indulge in fine Italian dining at Mosconi, renowned for its authentic flavors and exquisite pasta dishes. The restaurant's elegant ambiance adds to the overall dining experience.

2. Clairefontaine: For a taste of Luxembourgish cuisine with a modern twist, Clairefontaine offers a sophisticated dining setting. Enjoy creatively crafted dishes made from locally sourced ingredients.

3. La Pomme Cannelle: Located in a historic building, La Pomme Cannelle provides a charming atmosphere for French-inspired cuisine. The menu features a variety of delicacies, and the restaurant is known for its excellent service.

4. Um Plateau: Experience Luxembourg's culinary diversity at Um Plateau, offering a fusion of international flavors. The menu showcases creative dishes that appeal to a broad range of tastes.

5. Chocolate House Nathalie Bonn: Indulge your sweet tooth at the Chocolate House Nathalie Bonn, a haven for chocolate lovers. From decadent desserts to hot chocolate, this spot is a delightful treat for your senses.

6. Le Bouquet Garni: Enjoy a gastronomic journey at Le Bouquet Garni, where the chef's inventive creations showcase a blend of European and Mediterranean influences. The restaurant's intimate setting adds to its charm.

7. House of Wines Scott's Pub: If you appreciate wine and a relaxed pub atmosphere, House of Wines Scott's Pub is the place to be. With an extensive wine list and hearty pub fare, it's perfect for a casual evening.

These dining spots offer a diverse range of culinary experiences, from traditional Luxembourgish dishes to international delights, ensuring a memorable gastronomic journey in Luxembourg.

Here are 7 crucial phone numbers to know:

1. Emergency Services:
   - Police, Fire, Medical Emergency: **112**

2. Luxembourg City Tourist Office:
   - General Inquiries: **+352 22 28 09**

3. Public Transportation Information:
   - Luxembourg City Transport (Mobilitéitszentral): **24 65 24 65**

4. Medical Assistance:
   - Emergency Medical Service: **112**
   - Luxembourg Red Cross: **+352 2755-1**

5. Lost or Stolen Credit Cards:
   - Visa: Check the back of your card for the specific number.
   - MasterCard: Check the back of your card for the specific number.

6. Airport Information:
   - Luxembourg Airport: **+352 24 64 0**

7. 24/7 Embassy Emergency Line:
   - In case of issues involving your home country, contact your embassy's emergency line. Find this number on your embassy's website or at the embassy itself.

Make sure to have these numbers accessible during your stay in Luxembourg for a safe and enjoyable trip.

7 unknown facts about Luxembourg:

1. Multilingual Nation: Luxembourg has three official languages: Luxembourgish, French, and German. The multilingual nature of the country reflects its cultural diversity.

2. Highest GDP per Capita: Luxembourg consistently ranks as one of the countries with the highest GDP per capita in the world. Its prosperous economy is driven by a strong financial sector.

3. Grand Duchy: Luxembourg is the only remaining Grand Duchy in the world. The head of state is the Grand Duke, currently Grand Duke Henri, and it has a constitutional monarchy.

4. Picturesque Castles: Despite its small size, Luxembourg boasts over 100 castles and fortresses. Vianden Castle, perched on a hill overlooking the Our River, is one of the most picturesque and well-preserved.

5. European Institutions: Luxembourg City is home to several European Union institutions, including the European Court of Justice, the European Investment Bank, and the European Court of Auditors.

6. Schengen Agreement Birthplace: The village of Schengen in Luxembourg is where the Schengen Agreement, which led to the creation of the Schengen Area with open borders, was signed in 1985.

7. Culinary Influences: Luxembourg's cuisine is influenced by both German and French culinary traditions. It features hearty dishes like Judd mat Gaardebounen (smoked pork neck with broad beans) and Gromperekichelcher (potato cakes).

These lesser-known facts add layers to Luxembourg's identity, showcasing its unique blend of history, culture, and economic strength.